HELL FIGURES

E. Tracy Grinnell

HELL FIGURES

Nightboat Books
New York

ISBN 978-1-937658-47-2

Design and typesetting by Margaret Tedesco
Text set in Helvetica Neue and Bembo

Original cover art by Ashley Lamb: (front cover) *Entrance Hall*;
(back cover) *The Fake Wedding*, 2015; collage, 11 x 8 inches

Cataloging-in-publication data is available
from the Library of Congress

Distributed by University Press of New England
One Court Street
Lebanon, NH 03766
www.upne.com

Nightboat Books
New York
www.nightboat.org

for my family, given and chosen

Chorus:
Oh for all the world a Helen!
Hell at the prows, hell at the gates,
hell on the men-of-war

Agamemnon, Aeschylus (trans. Robert Fagles)

war
made them all insane

Antigo Nick (Sophokles), (trans. Anne Carson)

CONTENTS

episode i.

Leukadia

All Sappho's music is lost.

If not, winter, Introduction, Anne Carson

heights I can't imagine   so I

drift into ether's

                                                    web

Helen, I

                                    slips
                                            in the trash

        then I
        though thou

        follow the swallow

        who dreamt of me

lost the landscape

       in wait for the sea to reach me

to a portrait then   forever

echo that won't echo

      light returns

     sight

in darker dreams   waves

manifest — limb from limb

as a lung crack'd

                from side to side

the crest hides my

sight, my eye, my —

acres to cover

in papers, films, rooms

leagues unravel

over bodies

resolved figures

THE END

tied to birds' wings

tied to me

bandaged by root-like

flying things

fear of death, pain

meaning one's own

voices that are vices

in deserts that are ruins

cities overlook soundscapes

barren avenues

wars that are hanged

languages

night doubles into lack of day

night's trouble, my double

      in paradise the tempest

      interior

to look through water

      dragged   to list again —

I don't even reach out —

breaking the surface would be

like reminiscing

bloodshed

the mirror is mired

in second sight

flashes of light   are to look

through   to think

what is it   while I gaze on it

reflections resolve by fugues

first will to see first

sight   a trace

consider the voice   a song

penetrates by its hardened core

painted whether that is land

or water   or weather

my landscape

        landlocked

no longer consumed

to break upon the boats below

before the mind that made them

                exists a lost construction

corridors, doors

            slips in
the   trash

as much a place and not

as anywhere

one has been nor

never been

as boneheaps blanch in sayings

grey-eyed to all completion

one's expression reflects

a face, a cage, a trace —

the objective   the eyes

follow   swallowing the world

there in its echo chamber

water-dark   sounding

each night a new leaf

a new night   each to each

        against the streets

given to muse   scared up

the chairs in suites

in airs

awake along the surface

as air that is water-mist

grates the cord   tender cut

chords   anti-spheres

against the face a force

imagines emerging

a tangled animal   crack'd

      by the mirror

and tangled lies beyond

      its tangled head

effigies move like paper

burns

a footfall first   before me

breaths are cast

a glance gasps for

the instrument hung

equal parts flame

       and branch   aloft   alight

the adventures of those whose eyes

        in palm   heart in head

violate   extortions   of a face

without astonishment

without even bridges to cross

all deafening   impossible

if the chasm were not a figure

its own memory

in time   in night

        the two twisted   in half

light or its lack — a bloom

the canvas eats

everything for throes

only sometimes calm

the tempest interior   takes

the tragic calm of acrobats

brief, injurious to the stars

and everyone

wandering above   weighted

      below   that   wasting place

               eaters, thrushes, bearers

pools of millions   that ecstasy of —

   ones who do and those

       — who are done

I remember the anodyne

for my own inventions

the insinuation I pale

for death without sentences

there is the air

as one waits for things

ruts reopen, channels, gullies

dim shapes, new ghosts

      swallows

swallows in numbers

to float a soul?   nameless

      to be   childless

blood and the flower

in the shape of the blood

        reflecting no further

precipice or prophesy

the effigy imagines us

panoptic glass eye

the shadow breaks

the illumination is the illusion

a narrow flight

an arrow mirrors

flame or flight   sleeping

the surface

the corpse —

upgaze, the armor, the amour

so close as a torrent   if in the water   dark

closes a throat

to cover one's ears   lashed

to what is left   re-sounding

the very eye leaves

      liquid   the mirage

rings hollow   for all the eye

ravishes in shade   of the crest

each to each

unknown

to say *there is no way*

then *which way*

the body concusses the senses

a familiar illusion

is none, nobody —

what confession?

all while eyes receive

ears are useless

beneath the surface

another surface doubles the skin

a horizon we cannot make

in a world without —

but *I do live*

in that great deep   that dying

lake   a monumental sarcophagus

I cannot pry

even memory's

                    overtakelessness

I dissect the little fish that glide

around my hands to prove

they live   to ask of them

a prophesy:

what shall I pry at

you little fish?

if there is   never again

time   or figure   or the boundary

                              perhaps where

the beasts have wings, the lungs

                              the wars

— limb from limb —

if then I —   though thou

    follow the swallow   the shattering

the imagination   into weightlessness

    of a portrait's gaze

others of the apparition   beat the beast

with its own wings?

they leave me

thrown shrouds

their arms   their shadowed

their membranes all   wind–lashed to me

torn from a *trompe-l'œil*

given up for gone

how easy to find   deserted plains

full of   desirous   views

earth far from —   from —

how the horizon reclaims the voyager

now conveyed awhile among the weathers

who is it, now alone amidst the sea?

Humoresque

Cassandra:
I know that I am mad,
but Mother, dearest, now, for this one time
I do not rave.

The Trojan Women, Euripides (trans. Edith Hamilton)

Only an ear to the sea, confided

error, swallowed whole in reflection, dream leaves

genuflecting, lovers return the one who

feeds the horizon

I, my only city erratic violence

I, my only compass is into the night–

like transfigured ocean, so seriously

operatic, *I*

Waves seem seamless, water of memory comes
nearer naught alliteration serves night, dead
ringers delight favoring muses' rapture
battling sirens

Sea to sea remembers succumbing to sea

light's horizon-song undone, lyre unmasked far

depths, Lydonia's canyon in darkened straits while

as if there, as if —

Moreso silent falling, lacunae like laps

calling, where my body unmooring, false hull

nor my carriage go, nor my wayward vessel

nor listen to gulls

Foreign skin, I, bedded in waxwood, root-like

tearing hold-fasts, finger-long fishlets *caw-caw*

at my eardrums drowning, unable, I list

all that I look on

Rebellious bird of uncommon waters

I am what is bested, the beast and all, by

violins, the lyre, or whatever cursed love

fixes in triumph

Overhead the listing embodied, blind touch

black ocean, figures solve nothing, every house falls

eventually — perpetual motion, wild light

seaworthy false knell

Terror of bodies, swelling the ocean's blank stare

comely night, catastrophe's bidding for each

hawking failures of fantasy, ghosts of restless

slaughtering tongues wail

Empty terrain proffering expiration

bated promontory's reflection echoes

acres of sirens, deviants confounding war–

lords in every dream

Captive captor, whispering times unleashed

faceless songs of tangled instruments tempest

prone to tidal violence, counting octaves'

breathless precision

Droning, soundless, everywhere watching, what eyes?

nothing betrayed my dying archaic smile, that

one loves best a warrior's coma, thronging

empty, relenting

Crisis lyrics frozen, forever in arms

false reflections leaping to render fragments

whole, a promontory of gazes gone to

prosopopoeia

Growing cold or fearsome, the darkness of earth

offers what? a palindrome's logic, false glass

ricochet, reversal is reminiscent

pacing in cages

Gentle cushions, water of wings unfurling

only glassless while unemployed, the mirror

mars its mirror, faceless until it's gazed on

wits gone to wander

Tonight I think I die in filmy advances

lucid ocean begins again, untoward

figures' bird–like cants — who knows what it is to

perish in nonsense

episode ii.

Helen, A Fugue

Helen:
A name can travel where a body can't.

Helen, Euripides (trans. James Michie and Colin Leach)

For if she flees, soon she will pursue

If not, winter, Sappho (trans. Anne Carson)

My mouth a servant
a mirror dreamed

landscape written
another tongue

the auspices cry —
visionary reversals

in flight, phantoms delight
— let the betting begin!

Part I

Blood pools
in the roiling ocean

    futures
to fathom, where there is nothing

        even a pregnancy, is
feverish, I secretly

        , beyond fantasy
ambition follows

in a figure, my

  gestation
whirlwinds

in flight, a footprint falls

like nostalgia
        at first a sensation

your gaze
I think

by my own tongue

above
in suspended animation

suspended from
a flying thing, tied
to it

as thought, the sea
a score
breaks, an eye casts

lambs are alms
palms shot through

by the blue
the proverbial number
rushes
throng in swansea, I happen to be dying
in, words

Part II

The echo that watches
listens, meshes

of noon
in travels

released from origins
resist were I to

, turned, what keeps
you, split in two

, the doubled world
in all its doting
on my every *tête-à-tête*

letters fall on vacant lots
circling — *caw-cawing*

roses of muses
in ruses I, even I
           to phantoms
every limb, armed

the air, the aura
the ell-shaped mouths

of arcadian girls

certain slants
of their severed souls

taught to sing, in
siren scales

, immersed,
by ear, by rote, or travels abroad

bird-serpent
serpent-bird

what makes of me
any Hermione

serpent-mouthed
speaking back

Where heat
or anarchy, beat

affinities animate
the animal, lying
, residue of my foreign tongue

gasps cloister
my armory, the crowds
, sacrificial birds, render
re-member

what thought, was flying
turreted my

           contrary feeling
myth itself

armor, a name in name

my own, in name
          travels where
, no body

letters alone
proliferate

I, my letters
          in absence of

fastening fast, furied
lambs for

loudening illusion
, fall falsely

how else traverse
, in loudening

howls the rendered
animal,

darkest, darkening
refraction, our

       how else
stand, walk, murmur, think
, grieve?

Silence mouths
of, unmoving
, mouth, marked
darkened, where I
catch my own

but their echoes
are transfigured rituals
hurried through

repetition, cyclical
myth–time, in this

I am a tree
amid threats
of war!

intervals of changing
figures, fix
, history fugues

       the fairer
cloaked in songs

more fortunate, the sea

its faceless

kingdom's come
, run aground

traced, or
embodied, every

instance
, exemplary body
count

bloodlines pool, within
a shroud, that shifts

skulking
in, a settled score

sounds
, afterimages of
eyes, open–shut

       travels to air
turn to air, to swan
, no–name, to birth

Part IV:

Tongues, I
throttle among

      , my
limbs are, thumbs
phantom-fleeing, succumbing
, upon reflection

shots rung out
in lines, of image-
shapes

convictions made, of stones
, pebbles,   unturned, the urns
burn

follow my,
city, pursue

        , body-figures
, cut and calloused
my, pyre

flood, swallows
, gone

messages slant from
rubble, trapped just, quartets

, as if,
the end of time

disaster's animals
restrained, in rooms
facing

whatsoever the dark,
earth, loves

        returns, from it
every front line, rendered

lost what's, all
is, what I lay
, here

the walls shall have it all

cloaked in songs, the brawls
hereafter, the place, I
, no more identify, than love, I
the undersigned

Bloodied, whose
hands, this

figure no more

whether in contrary
motion, to
, projections, turn

to stand fast, the gate

fury hums, hurried
disastrous, appearances
, dismember

veils for though, I

visionary dis–
integration, thought

for nought, for all
what is cruel
, is cruel

feverish to,
even as it fades
it fails

to veil, in vanishing

its own disappearance
forgets its own

shattered shell
, mother bones

grey–hearted, eye
concrete sky, in secrecy
, despising, I

collapses every, speaking
   , tower — songs, the naming
rushes — *sssssshhhhh* — say

remains, my eyes, my
   animal dreams, over and
    , over, like washing, vanishing

In this very night
a movement, of

to seek a sequential self

thought as earth that changes the sea
changes the fishes, in it

my self, my self, my very very self
interred, to

sea as blood, earth, a death
    bed,   and,
        every other use, in me

                the fortunes of landscapes
in the fantasies of architecture

the discrepancy double exposures
casts of light crack time

canvas of time
moves my other,

from here the world
is wrought
heads I shuffle among

mirrors

those, false frontiers

move to

, mimic the figures, that I

        mimics

flees, it pursues, its

        swan the swan the singing swan

dying, floating
swan, no swan

that is no swan, boiling
raining, swan, as

       long gone
swan,   raped what imprint
left to imprint on

the perfect swan
eidolon, a doting
, swan

The reckless landscape's
counterpoint, hemmed in
at crossroads — the end of time
, hung swan

falling glass seems
musical
in the transparency

permeability
you dream, I dream

sky-inhabiting
grey-eyed
conundrum-wed

there is no birth
in your eyes

anguish-wild
whirlwind-footed

coming and going

like surfaces to souls
tied beating to a stake

what future is not bound
, thought

what bloodhound sought
the progeny

of facts, infamous, I
neglect them like every,
normalcy

      not dawn, not dusk, daylight,
  or night

     , into the
singing marginalia
to, the inside

I am bound, fastened
and fluttering

for my own sake, and

episode iii.

The Birds

Chorus:
Entities without wings, insubstantial as dreams,
you ephemeral things, you human beings:
Turn your minds to our words, our ethereal words,
for the words of the birds last forever!

The Birds, Aristophanes

Servant:
There never was any sense in watching sacrificial flames
and listening to the cries of birds —

Helen, Euripides (trans. James Michie and Colin Leach)

THE BIRDS

I shall hardly read the mystery of your riddle

floating the shoreline like a habit

silent without voices, strings, winds

the eye like a moon — part of the weather is

your own, madness is what you see as nature turning against you

the eye like a moon — part of the weather is

silent without voices, strings, winds

floating the shoreline like a habit

I shall hardly read the mystery of your riddle

THE BIRDS

the terroir, of amnesia

no wind, and the grey sea calm and full

the sensation of not moving on a moving staircase

time unwound — episodic blur

in flight, disappeared where you know not, lost momentarily in

your own madness, is what you see as nature turning against you

in flight, disappeared where you know not, lost momentarily in

time unwound — episodic blur

the sensation of not moving on a moving staircase

no wind, and the grey sea calm and full

the terroir, of amnesia

is a rhyme, a repetition, or no reason

a throat closes, dying of words — *Sphinx*

from the Greek "to strangle"

an ecstatic mind becomes your own worst enemy and

your own madness is what you see, as nature turning against you

an ecstatic mind becomes your own worst enemy and

from the Greek "to strangle"

a throat closes, dying of words — *Sphinx*

is a rhyme, a repetition, or no reason

THE BIRDS

who does not know what it is to struggle in darkness

flocks of birds as light, their liquid lachrymose abundance

in eyebeams battering the landscape

cast chiaroscuro and kept at arm's length

your own madness is what you see as nature, turning against you

cast chiaroscuro and kept at arm's length

in eyebeams battering the landscape

flocks of birds as light, their liquid lachrymose abundance

who does not know what it is to struggle in darkness

THE BIRDS

wild, with the deft precision of machines, colourless as salt

pale and ashen as our futures — unstrung in the ebb

the surge of every accident in order, descending in spiral

a million years of memory culminates in a point, it moves

your own madness is what you see as nature turning, against you

a million years of memory culminates in a point, it moves

the surge of every accident in order, descending in spiral

pale and ashen as our futures — unstrung in the ebb

wild, with the deft precision of machines, colourless as salt

THE BIRDS

a sonorous animal moves with and within the landscape it also defines

is no more capable of turning *on* than *away*

sadness rearranged to madness that by nature's law

— to bend, to become — rends itself *into*

the order of disorder, riding the waves in a manner of waiting *out*

your own madness is what you see as nature turning against you

the order of disorder, riding the waves in a manner of waiting *out*

— to bend, to become — rends itself *into*

sadness rearranged to madness that by nature's law

is no more capable of turning *on* than *away*

a sonorous animal moves with and within the landscape it also defines

THE BIRDS

every river to the sea inclines us to go by kind

bound to the fears of our weathers

eventually deserted for each to each

of all for all to know

your own, madness is what you see as nature turning against you

of all for all to know

eventually deserted for each to each

bound to the fears of our weathers

every river to the sea inclines us to go by kind

vanishing point

A Woman:
We stand at the same point of pain.
You mourn your ruin,
and in your words I hear my own calamity.

The Trojan Women, Euripides (trans. Edith Hamilton)

What can I do?

in the narrow mirror
showing the part for all?

Confusing the halo for scattered light
this farce of love
I know
you know
the lost time
the midday alchemy
my knocking against the walls

open air, solitary
enough

for anguish upon
water, upon dirt
the air
the darkest night
a day that
will not
set

Brothers
most lost
sister
most near
brothers
most near
sister
most lost

change ringing
rings necks
the bell my ears upon
my head cry into

in subtitled intimations
       silent   flares, of open mouths —

          plied my eyes
      with glass   stain tears
      and to the sea in ships
the ones I'll never know

          swallowed me whole
with no air
     shut in to swing

Caught
on film:

it darkens

it carries

it flees

it hastens

it renders

it calls

it tends

it marks

it echoes

it comes

it arms

it loosens

it shadows

it makes

it draws

it unravels

it overruns

it won't

it suffocates

it silences

it gives

it alters

it shatters

it is

it follows

it lingers

it senses

it rebels

it inhabits

it lights

it wants

it escapes

it haunts

it veers

it tears

it masks

it shudders

it opens

it rises

it burns

it ties

it swings

it weeps

it leaves

it buries

it empties

Sympathies of musculature

    equal the last wave
        of a mother's grip

a contortionist's key
seems concrete —

    wandered among the swamps, rushes
battered by
    an argument of wings

    the wandering
  is against understanding

    every aviary consumes
the argument:

what hangs, for what act

what stands in for hanging

    what intention

      inflection

such fractions of a view
troubled into
       revelations

that the abstract, dreams
       are also limited —

       expression
is to touch
as someone
is to sight

there — and there
again —

neither the memory unhinge
neither my heart
from her shell

Clocks chant
in the strangest ocean

to each echo, the foil
a face immured

therefore the trespasses
the place to end

come out   *come out*

this —
the inability —

                 — *déshabiller*

the habit
of mirrors
in reflection
on bodies
of water —
              the future

              so amused
under rapture

while attentions
revise themselves
fall to sleep

mouth
florid lines
flushed conceits
of the skin

Along the internal horizon
the rim erupts,
                    oracular fumes
form the fissure

                    if the air
the reflective body
hammers out
gives way

a dying thrush
beats about the head
          thrushing because
it's dying

its wings are winds
scaring up the humors
held
behind one mask
                    another

that I want
to kill these sentiments
like so many fruits
of a deserted womb — they are
disloyal, arrogant

    temptations to return and then
to torment

        instrumentality
is the cold wind, revenge
a labor
  pain, a folly
about to tell the world
      my folly
      is my pain

cloud–dissuaded
carried off —

tyranny — that other state — the sea
from some surface
desires surface

the entry to hell fills me
with
        hope —

preferable to strings
tongues to corsets
stopped mouths
unhinge, the gate
the pursuer
      the want that wants
only more

    and no shape yet to tell

  there are
the obstacles
the shadows

one's own deceptions
for oneself

the ends
      hanged
for retrospection

      one's own blood self-selects
for survival
  the chagrin of empires
    in trumpet swans

Bells
ring out
sound
            surveys
its own
  sound–blindness

simultaneous to all
            violence
so that every sense rebels
save my jealous ear

        views suffer
into the invariable
vanishing
            divided
                into
                        unencumbered
silence
            every
            face
    I try
      rattles the very membrane
            of our perpetual separation

    so that it hardens, like a bell
rings out

what we borrow
from the world —

    rumored
arrested
        — eaten away

the voyage
    vocalized, low in the shade
carried out — rollers over
our mutable landscape

the bravado
the use

on arrival
another enclosure for

    the noise
the list
the first forgotten

— flightless
in flight —
        the freefall

[*Que me veux-tu?*, 1929
            Gelatin silver print
            18 x 23 cm
            Claude Cahun   ]

episode iv.

between the figures and the elsewhere[i]:
notation as relation[ii]

The time of the composition is the time of the composition.
It has been at times a present thing it has been at times a past
thing it has been at times a future thing it has been at times
an endeavor at parts or all of these things.

"Composition As Explanation," Gertrude Stein

All those interpenetrations which seem at first glance to be hellish…
are to be espoused.

Silence, John Cage

That is, we order falsely when we summarize and explain,
a hierarchical contruct which conceals relation.

How Phenomena Appear to Unfold, Leslie Scalapino

"as subject in a constant state of replacement
concentric stages of loss and replacement:"[iii]

*looking at Sappho, or rather the Leukadian cliff from which she
is said to have leapt — the "lover's leap" — artist becomes subject.
seeming at once to fall, float, and fly as she leaps —

         peri-poet[iv]   [

         ]
        [*Sapho se précipitant dans la mer*, 1880
                  Watercolor
                  33 x 20 cm
                  Gustave Moreau   ]

      Mnemosyne

              drowned in her own waters —

             "La sirène succombe à sa propre voix"[v]

if the memory
only of
a closed throat

of blue–
green

of liquid
of the mouth

but art describes fascination and —[vi]

★born of refractions, false reflections, and failed conjectures

★and died
in death, the briefest —

sea succumbing to sea[vii] /
liebestod[viii]

instrumentality of love, or
death /   humoresque[ix]

sapphic[x] /   akin to the tension of molecules
that forms the surface of
the sea

I gayly threw my effeminate body
into the flames unremittingly
but the entry to hell fills me

                              with hope /
                              "l'entrée de l'enfer me fut sans ésperance"[xi]

to throw the innocents
aloft —
I trust our poor ambitions
like catastrophes
etched definitively[xii]

                              where agency abandons
                              by whom
                              by what force, or system

                                                  but to concede★

instrumentality[xiii]

              where ever
              whom ever
                  appears exists   regardless   to have
        been a force
        in time   is still

(*— elements at odds — draw the eye — and among
— reflections —
proliferate, pool, further into
— projections —
each

La poesie garde son secret livre son secret garde son secret livre son secret[xiv]

utterance besieged
— at the moment —
of utterance

"will what she invoke
destroy her?"[xv]

multivocal echo chambers —
— the striking —
word for deep sleep:[xvi]
threshold of speech
— madness — ecstasy —
fugue)

at once speaking, silent & absent

"Leads a double life. The vanishing point. Like zero. You agree
the point represents, within the physical scene, a definite location.
Location, however, vanishing toward the infinite. Your reaction to
this distance is wind blowing across frozen plains."[xvii]

(the "Silent Part" is just that: silent.
A performer would seem to sing, mouthing words
operatically and emotively
but as if —
behind glass)

[*Sapho tombant dans le gouffre*, 1867
Oil on panel
20 x 14 cm
Gustave Moreau   ]

"what you see in the rear-vision mirror isn't normal"[xviii]

— looking glass —
looking back   [

]   what do you want from me?

the body forms
a second skin[xix]

this the inability

déshabiller

the idea engenders the existence, love precedes the organs[xx]

in the streams of history —
the body with no voice
is terror —

"The agency by which the sea was dried up / was a 'strong east wind.'"[xxi]

an image resolves — to try to see the parts— in focus—the place,
the *I* — determination
of / at
the promontory

a compositional / psychological state[xxii]

the fugue is eight fours — following a pattern of beats, in the
theatrical sense, or phrases, in the musical one — parts assigned one
or two voices, enabling variation and doubling —

the sequence a palindrome[xxiii]

beside / before / around
to catch the throwing back of light — or heat —
concentration of thought?

one and two beats in one breath / four
and eight in two

Aloysius. Fugue takes its name from the words *fugere* and *fugare* — to
flee and to pursue[xxiv]

"at some point, or at gunpoint
human is to wander"[xxv]

            wind blowing across frozen plains — the poem falls —
        a sheet over furniture — pre-structures brace the poem —
      forms / phrases / mythologies / languages / internal systems
                        at work beneath — in concert —

"each figure explodes, vibrates in and of itself like a sound severed
from any tune — or is repeated to satiety, like the motif of a
hovering music"[xxvi]

                literal form / mood-as-form
                      / as architectural elements

                    /akin to the tension of
                    molecules / forms
                  the surface of the sea

beats are marked by stanza breaks and are observed as silences
commas and caesura are rhythmic indicators
the duration of silences may be freely determined but should be
consistent relative to one another

in wars of possession
deviants suicide /

/ or burn

"we are dependent on accidents of transmission — fire, war, loss"[xxvii]

[*La mort de Sapho*, 1872
                    Oil on canvas
                    81 x 62 cm
                    Gustave Moreau   ]

"there is an invisible architecture often supporting the surface of the
poem… its object is to possess the poem for a brief time, even as an
apparition appears…"[xxviii]

my sweet /

/ sweet, but at last /

in the end / at last!

/light rebels/

"the transition from the stability and absoluteness of the world's contents to their dissolution into motions and relations"[xxix]

All works, I venture, are written *after.* [xxx]

NOTATION

[i] *The Vulgar Tongue*, Norma Cole

[ii] "between the figures and the elsewhere: notation as relation" was prompted by an exchange with Bhanu Kapil and first published as "A Peripoetext to Accompany Leukadia" in the chapbook *Leukadia* (Trafficker Press, 2008)

[iii] *The Vulgar Tongue*, Norma Cole

[iv] operating within and/or via ecstasy — from the Greek *ekstasis*: [to be put out / of place] outside or beside oneself in states of passion, rage, grief, astonishment — as exposure, consciousness, trance. the companion is also oneself: simultaneous — outside / beside / around

[v] *Aveux non avenus*, Claude Cahun

[vi] from *Hell and Lower Evil* (Lyre Lyre Pants on Fire Press, 2008), a homophonic translation of "Hélène la rebelle" by Claude Cahun

[vii] Sappho's sexuality has been sufficiently troubling to generations of poets, critics, and scholars (learned men) that a myth was introduced into her biography, to make of her an example: deviants suicide. There is no way, no where, for disastrous desire.

[viii] *Tristan und Isolde*, Richard Wagner

[ix] Antonin Dvorák

[x] - u - x - u u -   u - - / - u - x - u u -   u - - / - u - x - u u - u - - / - u u - u

[xi] *Aveux non avenus*, Claude Cahun

^{xii} from *Hell and Lower Evil*

^{xiii} a theatrical crossiNg
                from lefT to right
            so slowly as to sEem to be
                moviNg
                    noT at all
            the musIc meanwhile
        as fast as pOssible...

                thUs
                a Canvas
                of Time is provided
                                "Composition in Retrospect," John Cage

^{xiv} *Les paris sont ouverts*, Claude Cahun

^{xv} *Helen in Egypt*, H.D.

^{xvi} [kōma]

^{xvii} *Driven to Abstraction*, Rosmarie Waldrop

^{xviii} *versary*, Kate Lilley

^{xix} we need to be conscious of an ongoing tension between our desire to
register fragmentation and our desire to invent integrity.
                                Sappho Is Burning, Page DuBois

^{xx} action or instrumentality. where agency seems not to exist, instrumentality.
alights. and what is the difference? female figures of artistic creation, prophecy,
ingenuity / stripped / of identity, sanity & voice

144

xxi OED: *c1854* STANLEY *Sinai & Pal.* i. (1858) 35

xxii Though "Helen, A Fugue" was written in 2008 before I had read M. NourbeSe Philip's *Zong!* it is impossible to ignore the deep formal resonance in the use of the fugue, and so I gesture to that simultaneity, the *coming to* about which she writes.

xxiii 8421   4218   2184   1842   2481   4812   8124   1248
Part I   Part II   Part III   Part IV   Part VI   Part III   Part II   Part I

xxiv "Fugues in General," Johann Josef Fux

xxv *The Vulgar Tongue,* Norma Cole

xxvi *A Lover's Discourse,* Roland Barthes

xxvii *Sappho Is Burning,* Page DuBois

xxviii *Forces of Imagination,* Barbara Guest

xxix *Commons,* Myung Mi Kim

xxx

Dear Leslie,

Early this morning, I dreamt I was in the *Twilight Zone* episode "The Eye of the Beholder" (first titled "The Private World of Darkness"), trying to see through the glass and gauze floating in front of my face. In the episode, Miss Janet Tyler (played by Maxine Stuart) is in a hospital, her face covered with bandages, having undergone multiple surgeries to correct a hideous deformation that has made her life in society impossible. She has had her final operation, this is her last chance, and if it has failed to correct the deformation she will be sent to live in exile in a village with others like her — others deemed hideous by the State. I remember reading at some point that they filmed parts of this episode from Miss Tyler's perspective by placing a camera inside a fish bowl wrapped in gauze. In my dream, I was inside the fish bowl, looking out as though from her perspective, my vision obstructed with only the slightest hints of light breaking through the gauze. Of course, this isn't *her* perspective, since she isn't inside the bowl, rather, it is the perspective of the camera recording the experience of blindness, of sight deprivation and conveying disorientation and anxiety. Waking from the dream, I found myself thinking this is somehow an analogy for homophonic translation, or perhaps more broadly, the process of writing these poems through the ciphers of mythological and historical female figures.

When writing *Hell and Lower Evil*, a homophonic translation of Claude Cahun's *Hélène la rebelle*, I was attempting to avoid a semantic translation (in spite of a familiarity with the French language) of Cahun's work, using visual and acoustic association to render a new version of the text. The visual / acoustic translation happening before sense is made in the mind's eye — an exercise in sens/ory deprivation akin to automatic writing — so that an altered sense is created:

"Je sais bien qu'il ne me désire même pas"
"gesture being killed / nemesis desiring my own past"

and in places, departing from the text, set on a path that falls away:

"Il nous faut, dans les faubourgs de Sparte, une maison de campagne, des enfants, le repos."
"it no more false / denies the false / bards of Spartan means / decampment, desperate infants / of late repose // in night / in night / pulse / might rebel its / episodic fugue-logic…"

A "hostage of fate" (*Tiger at the Gates*, Jean Giraudoux), Helen of Troy is a devastating vision/ary whose beauty is destruction itself. As a symbol of the folly of pride and arrogance, and of the disaster of going to war for an illusion, Helen is a projection that doesn't cease to travel — "a name can travel where a body can't" (*Helen*, Euripides) — and is therefore prophetic. The voice that emerges out of the non-sense in *Hell and Lower Evil*, resembles, or re-assembles, Frankenstein-like, "Hélène la rebelle," and is a recording of dissociation, conveying the acute disorientation of a no-man's land between languages, across time, between the moment of action and the reception of the perception of that action. This is a "terribly clairvoyant" Helen, speaking in tongues, revivified and calling out her own projection, inherently other. As a "hostage of fate," Helen has no agency, can only ever be a projection, never herself. Her vantage point is a vanishing point. We are left holding the projections, so devastatingly our own.

We find at the end of "The Eye of the Beholder" that
the corrective surgeries have failed, but when Miss Tyler
is unveiled (now played by Donna Douglas... a more
"attractive" actor?), we see that she is in fact "beautiful." It
is the faces — only shown in shadow and silhouette until
this point — of the doctors, nurses, and the State's leader,
speaking fanatically on T.V. about conformity, that are
deformed and misshapen.

written to Leslie Scalapino for *War & Peace 4: Vision*
January 25, 2009

ACKNOWLEDGMENTS

Exceptional gratitude for poetic engagement, conversation, and encouragement during the long progress of this work to Stefani Barber, Andrew Beccone, Rachel Bers, Norma Cole, Marisa Fuentes, Isabelle Garron, Judith Goldman, Brenda Iijima, Paul Foster Johnson, erica kaufman, Kathleen Miller, Laura Moriarty, Erin Morrill, Stephen Motika, Akilah Oliver, Trace Peterson, Leslie Scalapino, Stacy Szymaszek, Chris Warrington, Craig Watson, Tom White, and Richard K. Winslow. Also to Ashley Lamb for creating original artwork for the cover of this book and to Christian Hawkey and Rachel Levitsky for crucial feedback during the final stage of revisions.

I am also deeply indebted to the Millay Colony for providing me with the time and space necessary to complete some of these pieces and to conceive of the final structure of the manuscript.

Hell Figures was in process from 2005 through 2015. Thanks to the editors who published early versions, excerpts, notes, drafts, and sections of this manuscript:

Limited edition / chapbook publications: *Humoresque* (Blood Pudding Press / Dusie Collective #3, 2009); *Leukadia* (Trafficker Press, 2008); *Hell and Lower Evil* (Lyre Lyre Pants on Fire Press, 2008); Excerpt from *Helen, A Fugue* (included in The Belladonna Elder Series, Volume #1, Belladonna, 2008)

Journal / magazine publications: *Jacket 40, A Tonalist Section*, 2010; *Poets for Living Waters*, 2010; *War & Peace 4*, Oakland, CA, 2009; *New Review of Literature*, Los Angeles, 2008; *Boog City Portable Boog Reader*, New York, 2007; *Coconut*, 2007; *Van Gogh's Ear*, Paris, France, 2007; *EOAGH: Queering Language*, 2007

E. TRACY GRINNELL is the author of *portrait of a lesser subject*, *Music or Forgetting*, and *Some Clear Souvenir*. *Helen: A Fugue* was published in the first volume of the Belladonna Elders Series in conversation with *A Pear / Actions are Erased* by Leslie Scalapino. Grinnell's poetry has been translated into French, Serbian, and Portuguese. She currently teaches in the MFA Writing Program at Pratt Institute and lives in Brooklyn, New York. She is the founding editor and director of Litmus Press.

NIGHTBOAT BOOKS

Nightboat Books, a nonprofit organization, seeks to develop audiences for writers whose work resists convention and transcends boundaries. We publish books rich with poignancy, intelligence, and risk. Please visit our website, www.nightboat. org, to learn about our titles and how you can support our future publications.

The following individuals have supported the publication of this book. We thank them for their generosity and commitment to the mission of Nightboat Books:

Elizabeth Motika
Benjamin Taylor

In addition, this book has been made possible, in part, by grants from the National Endowment for the Arts and the New York State Council on the Arts Literature Program.

State of the Arts

NYSCA

ART WORKS.

National
Endowment
for the Arts
arts.gov